W9-CPF-673

J
612.82
EINSPRUC

6115

**Please check all items for damages
before leaving the Library.
Thereafter you will be held
responsible for all injuries
to items beyond reasonable wear.**

Helen M. Plum Memorial Library

Lombard, Illinois

A daily fine will be charged for
overdue materials.

JUN   2014

612.82
EIN

Published in 2014 by The Rosen Publishing Group, Inc.
29 East 21st Street, New York, NY 10010

Copyright © 2014 Weldon Owen Pty Ltd. Originally published in 2011 by Discovery Communications, LLC

Original copyright © 2011 Discovery Communications, LLC. Discovery Education™ and the Discovery Education logo are trademarks of Discovery Communications, LLC, used under license. All rights reserved.

All rights reserved. No part of this book may be reproduced in any form without permission in writing from the publisher, except by a reviewer.

Credits and acknowledgments
KEY tl=top left; tc=top center; tr=top right; cl=center left; c=center; cr=center right; bl=bottom left; bc=bottom center; br=bottom right; bg=background

CBT = Corbis; DT = Dreamstime;
iS = istockphoto.com;
SH = Shutterstock; TF = Topfoto; TPL = photolibrary.com

1c iS; 2tr SH; 2-3tc iS; 4-5cl iS; 8tr DT; 8-9bc SH; 9tc TPL; 10bc, br, br DT; bc iS; 12tr iS; tl SH; 12-13c DT; 13br, c iS; tc SH; 14cr iS; 14-15bl iS; 15bc, tr DT; tc, tc, tl iS; 16cr iS; 16-17bc iS; 17cr iS; br, tc SH; 18bc, bc, bc, bl, bl, bl, br, br, br, c, c SH; 19bc, bl, br DT; 20br DT; bl, tr iS; bc SH; 21tl CBT; br iS; bc, bl TF; 22tr CBT; bl iS; br TPL; 23tl iS; bl SH; br, br TF; tr TPL; 24bl SH; 25br iS; 26 bl, cr iS; cl SH; 26-27bg, tc iS; bc SH; 27tr DT; br iS; 28tr iS; bl, bl, br, br, cl SH; 29bl, c, cr SH; 30bg SH; 31bg SH

All illustrations copyright Weldon Owen Pty Ltd

Managing Director: Kay Scarlett
Creative Director: Sue Burk
Publisher: Helen Bateman
Senior Vice President, International Sales: Stuart Laurence
Vice President Sales North America: Ellen Towell
Administration Manager, International Sales: Kristine Ravn

Library of Congress Cataloging-in-Publication Data

Einspruch, Andrew.
 Brain works / by Andrew Einspruch.
     pages cm. — (Discovery education. How it works)
 Includes index.
 ISBN 978-1-4777-6305-6 (library) — ISBN 978-1-4777-6306-3 (pbk.) —
ISBN 978-1-4777-6307-0 (6-pack)
 1. Brain—Juvenile literature. 2. Nervous system—Juvenile literature. 3. Intellect—Juvenile literature. 4. Neurosciences—Juvenile literature. I. Title.
 QP376.E38 2014
 612.8'2—dc23
                         2013023134
Manufactured in the United States of America

CPSIA Compliance Information: Batch #W14PK2: For Further Information contact Rosen Publishing, New York, New York at 1-800-237-9932

3 1502 00784 2022

HOW IT WORKS

BRAIN WORKS

ANDREW EINSPRUCH

HELEN PLUM LIBRARY
LOMBARD, IL

PowerKiDS press.

New York

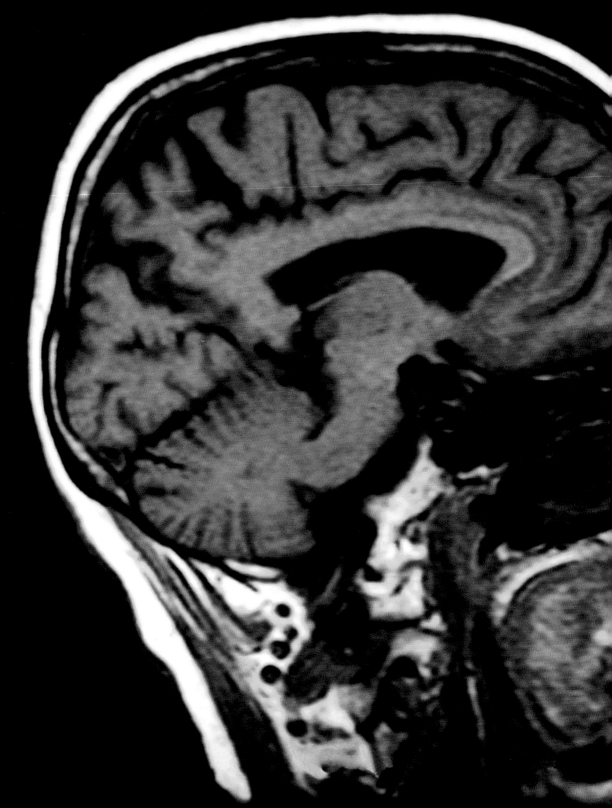

Contents

The Control Center

The brain acts as the control center for the body. It receives a constant flow of data about what is going on inside and outside the body via the senses. We are consciously aware of some of these signals, while others do not reach our consciousness at all.

The brain processes and makes sense of these sensory signals, and directs the body to act appropriately. It has specialized sections for handling different activities.

Primary motor cortex
This originates movements that a person consciously controls, which are called voluntary movements.

Primary somatosensory cortex
Information on touch, pressure, and pain is processed here.

Prefrontal cortex
You use this part to solve problems, express personality, emotions, and social behavior.

Broca's area
This section is involved in controlling speech and moving the body.

Wernicke's area
Language comprehension and the sounds that form speech relate to this area.

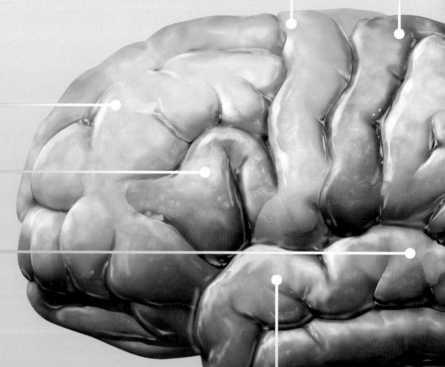

Cerebral cortex

Much of what humans think and do is controlled by the part of the brain called the cerebral cortex. This is divided into small sections with specialist functions.

Primary auditory cortex
This area is in charge of most of the sound processing, including pitch and loudness.

Different brains

Almost all animals have a head and a central nervous system, which includes a brainlike structure that connects to a nerve or a spinal cord.

Somatosensory association area
This interprets information from various senses so you recognize felt objects.

Angular gyrus
The processing needed for math, language, and understanding uses this part of the brain.

Visual association area
To recognize what you see, this area interprets visual data and relates it to past experience.

Primary visual cortex
Data from the eyes is received here to interpret shape, color, movement, and pattern.

Starfish
With no brain, the central nerve ring connects to nerves in each arm.

Nerve ring

Nerve

Salamander
This is one of the few animals that can repair a damaged spinal cord.

Brain

Spinal cord

Owl
The brain of an owl weighs only about 0.08 ounces (2.3 g).

Cerebrum

Cerebellum

Brain stem

Cat
The brain is organized in a similar way to an owl's and a human's.

Cerebrum

Cerebellum

Brain stem

Human
The human brain uses 20 percent of the body's energy.

Cerebrum

Cerebellum

Brain stem

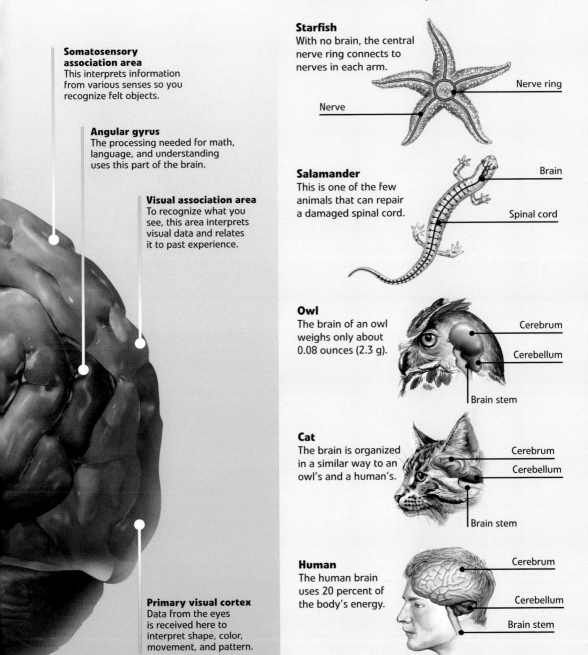

Inside the Brain

There are three main sections to the brain: the brain stem, the cerebellum, and the cerebrum. They form a kind of hierarchy in brain function, with the brain stem having the more basic functions and the cerebrum having the most complex.

The brain stem controls many survival functions, such as breathing and the beating of the heart. The cerebellum is in charge of balance, movement, and posture. The cerebrum, which is the largest section of the brain, is where thinking occurs. It takes in all the data relayed by the senses, processes and interprets it, then acts on it.

BASIC BRAIN STRUCTURE

The three main parts of the brain—the brain stem, cerebellum, and cerebrum—can be seen in this view of the brain from behind.

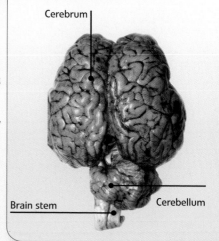

Cerebrum

Brain stem

Cerebellum

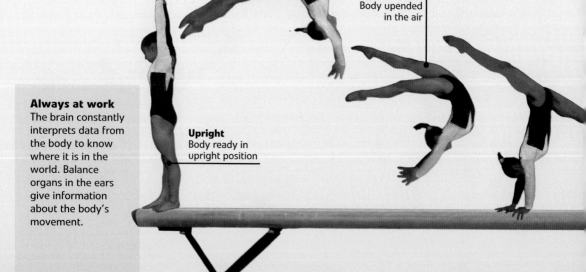

Upside down
Body upended in the air

Always at work
The brain constantly interprets data from the body to know where it is in the world. Balance organs in the ears give information about the body's movement.

Upright
Body ready in upright position

Complex mass of parts
The brain is made up of many parts that have very specific functions. Here are some of the brain's specialist parts.

Thalamus
It relays sensory data to the cerebral cortex, the outermost layer of the cerebrum.

Pituitary gland
At the base of the brain, this is the master gland of the endocrine system.

Cerebrum
The cerebrum has a folded outer layer called the cerebral cortex. Most data processing takes place there.

Cerebellum
This is smaller than the cerebrum and handles more basic bodily functions. It controls the body's movements.

Brain stem
Located deep inside the brain, the brain stem handles the most basic of bodily functions needed for survival.

An adult human's brain weighs about 3 pounds (1.4 kg). That is twice the weight of a giraffe's.

Upright again
Back in upright, balanced position

Airborne
Body moving through the air

Interneurons
(nerve cells) pass
along messages.

Brain

Spinal cord

The spinal cord
The spinal cord controls
the body's reflexes and
also acts as the conduit for
signals that pass between
the body and brain.

Vertebrae

HOW THE BRAIN WORKS

A simple action needs
a massive amount of
work and
coordination by the
brain, which gets all
of the parts of the
body cooperating to
take the action.

Decide
The prefrontal
cortex sends a
message to the
motor skills area.

Plan
The motor skills
area plans the best
path for the hand
to grasp the apple.

Pick up
The brain signals
the arm to move
and the hand to
pick up the apple.

Eat
The brain controls
the mouth opening,
teeth biting, and
chewing of the apple.

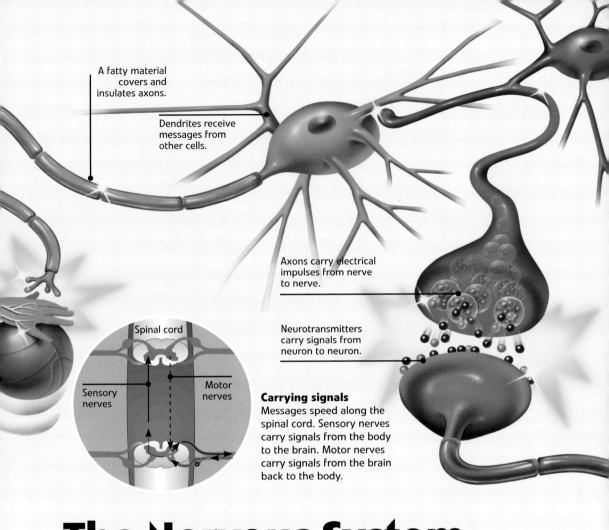

A fatty material covers and insulates axons.

Dendrites receive messages from other cells.

Axons carry electrical impulses from nerve to nerve.

Neurotransmitters carry signals from neuron to neuron.

Spinal cord

Sensory nerves

Motor nerves

Carrying signals

Messages speed along the spinal cord. Sensory nerves carry signals from the body to the brain. Motor nerves carry signals from the brain back to the body.

The Nervous System

The nervous system combines the brain with the spinal cord and all the nerves throughout the body. This creates a system that can sense what is going on in every part of the body. The nerves detect some kind of sensation. For example, the nerves in your fingers detect heat or pressure. The nerves then use electrical signals to pass that data up the spinal cord to the brain for interpretation, understanding, and action if it is needed.

Two nervous systems

The brain and spinal cord form the central nervous system. The nerves make up the peripheral nervous system, which connects all the body's organs and limbs to the central nervous system.

Mathematical puzzles
The analysis and logical step-by-step thinking that are needed to solve math puzzles are typically carried out by the left hemisphere.

Communicating
Verbal communication needs both sides of the brain: the left for grammar and vocabulary; the right for tone, accent, and understanding the context.

A PUZZLE FOR YOUR LEFT BRAIN

To solve the puzzle below, you will need to use your analytical abilities, which are typically controlled by the left side of the brain.

Who plays what?
Use the clues below to figure out which sport each child likes best.

1 Clare does not like animals or going in the water.

2 Ryan enjoys team sports and owns a helmet.

3 Katy's nickname is "the fish."

	Katy	Clare	Ryan
Swimming			
Polo			
Tennis			

Left and Right Ideas

Different areas of the brain control different functions. The cerebrum is also divided physically into left and right halves, called the left and right hemispheres. Some brain functions mostly occur in one or the other hemisphere. For example, logical reasoning and vocabulary are considered "left-brain functions." Creativity and dealing with new situations are more "right-brain functions."

Brain–body control
The left hemisphere controls the right side of the body. The right hemisphere controls the left side of the body.

Understanding jokes
The left brain recognizes the words in a joke. The right brain recognizes why the words combine to be funny.

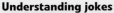

Fact or Fiction?
The left–right brain division is not as clear as it might seem at first glance. Many functions that people often think are on one side or the other are actually spread across both sides.

Being creative
Creativity involves dealing with new or different situations. It is considered a right-brain activity.

Corpus callosum
The corpus callosum connects the left and right hemispheres and lets both sides communicate with each other.

Mirror halves
The left and right cerebral hemispheres mirror each other exactly in their size and shape.

Map reading
Reading a map needs spatial understanding of the relation between objects in space. This makes it more of a right-brain task.

Rest for the Brain

Every part of the body needs rest, and the brain is no different. The brain never shuts down completely. If it did, the heart and lungs would stop working. Even so, sleep is a period of decreased brain activity, which lets the body focus on different functions. These include repairing itself, converting memories from short-term to long-term, and making mental connections.

The purpose of sleep is not completely clear. Many things go on in our body while we are asleep. But one thing is sure—getting enough sleep is key to physical and mental health.

Baby

16 hours

Sleep–deprived
When people do not get enough sleep, they are said to be sleep-deprived. They become irritable, lose their mental sharpness, and their health is affected.

HOW MUCH SLEEP IS ENOUGH?

The amount of sleep we need decreases as we get older. Babies need the most sleep (about 16 hours a day), but that amount is halved by the time we become adults.

Young child

10 hours

Adult

8 hours

Toddler

10-12 hours

Older child and teenager

9 hours

Whales and dolphins must consciously choose to breathe, so they can let only half their brain sleep at a time.

Occipital lobe
The occipital lobe is very active during sleep periods associated with dreaming.

Parietal lobe
If someone has damage to their parietal lobe, they may stop dreaming.

Frontal lobe
Its functions, such as speech and creative thinking, are affected by sleep deprivation.

Brain stem
It remains active because it controls survival functions such as breathing.

KEY
■ Reduced activity during sleep
■ Active during sleep

Brain activity
During sleep, the parts of the brain involved with staying alive and with dreaming remain active. Other parts slow down or contribute to dreaming.

Inherited or Learned?

S ome of our traits or personal qualities are inherited from our parents, while other traits are learned. Sometimes it is easy to tell whether a trait is inherited or learned, and sometimes it is not. Physical resemblance, for example, is inherited. When family members share physical characteristics such as hair color, eye color, height, or skin tone, these traits have been passed from parents to child through their genes.

But what about skill at sports or music? A child may inherit a natural talent, but to make the most of it requires many hours of learning and practice.

That's Amazing!

Your body has more than 20,000 genes, which control how you look, behave, and grow. Almost every cell in your body contains a complete set of your genes.

Inherited

A child can look like a combination of their parents because half of their genes come from their father and half of their genes come from their mother.

TWINS SEPARATED AT BIRTH

By looking at the lives of identical twins who grew up apart, scientists can study the influences of inheritance and learning. One famous study, started in 1979 by a team at the University of Minnesota, looked at 60 pairs of identical twins who were raised separately. The findings are not conclusive, but some of the twins had amazing similarities. An example of this is the "two Jims"—identical twins James (Jim) Arthur Springer and James (Jim) Edward Lewis. Separated when they were one month old, they met again when they were 39 years old.

Learned behavior

The more we practice something, the less it needs conscious thought. Firemen practice fighting fires so they can respond immediately when facing a fire. Musicians practice so their musical skills become automatic.

The two Jims

Both were called James by their adoptive parents.

Both married and divorced women named Linda, then married women called Betty.

Both liked mechanical drawing and carpentry.

Their favorite school subject was math.

Their least favorite was spelling.

Both smoked and drank the same amount and the same brands.

Both got headaches at the same time of day.

Both had dogs named Toy.

One had a son named James Alan. The other had a son named James Allan.

Identical twins have almost exactly the same genes. Genes of non-identical, or fraternal, twins are only 50 percent the same.

Memory

Memory is the brain's ability to store and retrieve information. If you had no memory, you would find it impossible to learn any facts or skills, or to change your behavior because of your experience or different circumstances.

Memories are not found in one part of the brain. They form as the brain's sensory processing areas interact with deeper areas. Short-term memories, like where you left your shoes, are stored briefly. More important memories, like the time you broke your arm, become long-term memories that remain for years.

SHORT-TERM MEMORY → **LONG-TERM MEMORY**

TIME AND PLACE **FACTS** **SKILLS**

How your memory works
Some short-term memories become long-term memories. Some are stored as facts (2 + 2 = 4). Others are motor skills (how to throw a ball) or events in your life (your fifth birthday).

That's Amazing!

Marc Umile recited a number 12,887 digits long. He remembered it by grouping two, four, and six digits together, and repeatedly listening to a recording of himself saying it.

Short-term memory test
Look at the picture below for 30 seconds and memorize as many objects as possible. Next, cover the picture and write down the names of all the objects you remember.

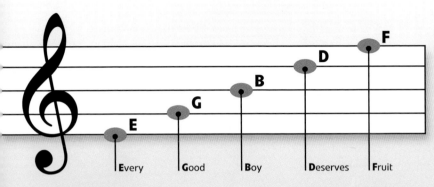

Mnemonic devices
Mnemonics are tricks to help memorize something. For example, the phrase "Every Good Boy Deserves Fruit" will help you recall these musical notes.

E — Every
G — Good
B — Boy
D — Deserves
F — Fruit

Memorize in chunks
If you can cluster things into chunks of information, they are easier to remember. For example, group a long number into small parts to memorize it.

Memorize this number
950634562

Memorize this number
867-3671-874

A MEMORY IN SLOW MOTION

1 The boy gets an ice cream cone, which acts as a stimulus to the senses.

2 Tasting the ice cream stimulates taste and touch senses. The neurons in the mouth send signals to the brain, and the flavor and feel of the ice cream are stored in the short-term memory.

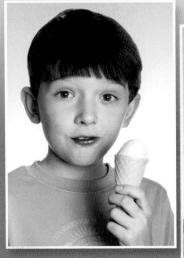

3 As the boy eats more ice cream, the short-term memory is transferred to the boy's long-term memory. He will remember it for years.

Brain Studies

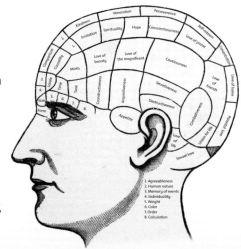

People have long wanted to know what goes on inside the brain. They have wondered how the mind works and how it and the brain connect to the body. The first known reference to the brain is in an ancient Egyptian text on treating illness from the seventeenth century BC. People have been studying the brain for thousands of years.

Today, scientists are getting closer to completely mapping the brain's activities. Using the latest technology, they can watch what happens in the brain when particular kinds of thoughts occur and when different types of activities are carried out. This gives us an insight into the human mind that earlier people could only have dreamed about.

Phrenology
The study of people's head shape to understand their personality traits was very popular in the 1800s.

LEONARDO DA VINCI

400 BC
Ancient Greeks thought the brain was the control center of the body. The physician Hippocrates believed it was related to the star sign Aries.

335 BC
The ancient Greek philosopher Aristotle believed the heart was the body's controlling organ, hence the expression "to learn something by heart."

AD 1452–1519
Leonardo da Vinci studied the human body, including the brain, by dissecting corpses. He drew diagrams of the brain from the dissected skulls.

BRAIN SCANS

An electroencephalogram (EEG) records the electrical activity that occurs when the brain functions. Activity shows as waves.

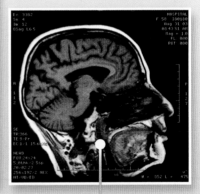

Alert

Relaxed

Drowsy

Asleep

Early brain surgery
Brain surgery dates back 9,000 years. Holes were drilled in the skull to treat seizures, migraines, and mental illness.

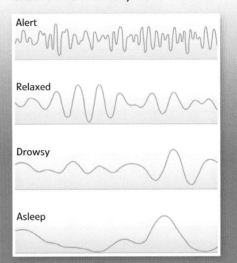

1861
Paul Broca (above), along with Carl Wernicke, identified parts of the brain related to speech. This proved specific processing tasks occur in specific brain areas.

1869–1939
Harvey Cushing pioneered neurosurgery. He used X-rays to locate brain tumors and developed surgical techniques for brain operations.

Today
With technologies such as magnetic resonance imaging (MRI), scientists are gradually improving their understanding of how the brain functions.

When Things Go Wrong

The brain is an extraordinarily complex organ, and many things can go wrong with it. Some mental disorders, such as certain phobias, are relatively mild. But brain disorders, such as Alzheimer's disease or a stroke, can be very debilitating for the person involved.

Many phobias and addictions can be cured. Some stroke patients recover much of their brain function. But other brain problems are permanent and change the person's life forever.

Bipolar disorder

This is also called manic depression. A person experiences intense mood swings from mania to depression and back. Vincent van Gogh, who painted this painting, probably suffered from it.

Depression

People who suffer from depression feel deep sadness and anxiety and lose their interest in life. Abraham Lincoln, the US president from 1861 to 1865, is known to have had depression.

Stroke

A stroke is a sudden decrease in brain function caused either by loss of blood flow to the brain or by bleeding in the brain. The damage can affect functions like speech or movement.

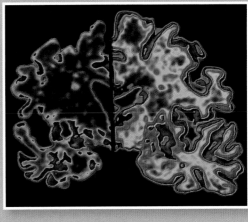

Addiction

The brain and body may become dependent on something, such as alcohol or drugs. Many also believe people can be addicted to habits such as gambling or watching television.

Alzheimer's disease

It starts with forgetfulness and progresses to increased confusion, mood swings, and severe memory loss. Brain changes include shrinking of the cerebral cortex (shown above on the left).

Parkinson's disease

This is the breaking down of the central nervous system. The sufferer loses control of movement, speech, and mental ability. Boxer Muhammad Ali has Parkinson's disease.

Phobia

A phobia is an irrational fear of a particular thing or situation, such as snakes, spiders, heights, or confined spaces. Many phobias can be treated so the person can live a normal life.

Brain Games

I f you understand how the brain works, then you can also figure out how to trick the brain. Optical illusions and other psychological games are a fun way to see whether or not your brain can correctly perceive and interpret things.

Some everyday experiences actually rely on the brain being tricked. Take movies, for example. What you see is a series of still images, but your brain strings them together so they appear to be one continuously moving image.

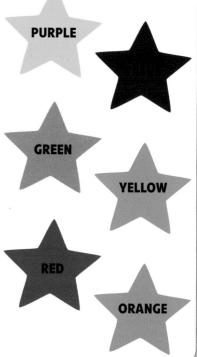

COLOR BRAINTEASER

As quickly as you can, say the color of each star. Most people have to slow down to get the color right, or they say the word inside the star, not the color.

PURPLE

BLUE

GREEN

YELLOW

RED

ORANGE

M. C. Escher
This Dutch artist was fascinated by illusions. He drew fantastic scenes rather than what he saw around him. These impossible scenes tricked or challenged the viewer's mind.

Which circle is larger?

If you chose the one on the left, then your mind has been tricked. The larger square makes you think the circle is also larger. Both circles are actually the same size.

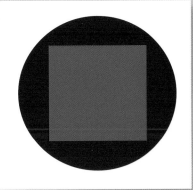

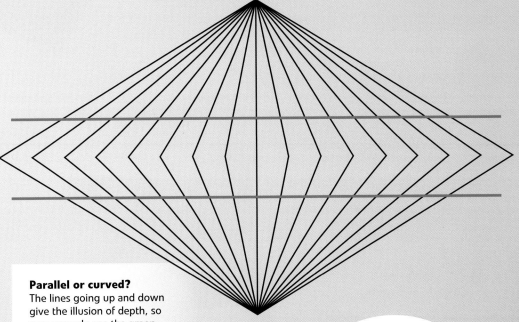

Parallel or curved?

The lines going up and down give the illusion of depth, so some people see the green bars as curving inward. But they are straight and parallel.

Optical illusions

The trick part of an optical illusion is often easier to spot if you cover part of the image. Try looking at only half the cube.

A Healthy Brain

The brain is like any part of the body—it needs to be kept healthy. That means exercising it, nourishing it, and protecting it from harm. This can be easy and fun. Puzzles and learning strengthen the brain. A healthy diet for the body as a whole is a healthy diet for the brain.

Sensible choices, such as putting on a safety helmet before riding a bicycle or a motorcycle, or wearing a seat belt in a car, help protect the brain from injury.

Safety
To protect your brain, protect your head. A helmet for cycling or baseball lowers the risk of brain injury if your head is hit.

Learning from others
Learning from others improves your skills and trains your brain. Talk to someone who knows something you do not.

Puzzles
One way to sharpen your mind is to solve puzzles. The more you do, the better you will get at them.

Sleep
Sleep is crucial. It lets the brain and body focus on nonwaking activities, such as healing and making mental connections.

Games

Like puzzles, games are another good way to stay sharp. Play different games so you work different parts of your mind.

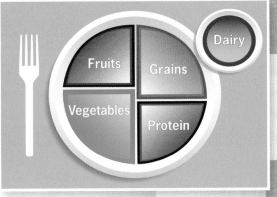

Health

Nourishing the body nourishes the brain. A healthy diet is important, with a focus on fresh vegetables and fruits. Also, be sure to get some exercise.

WIRED FOR RISK

The brains of young people are programmed for risk. This is because the prefrontal cortex—the part of the brain that controls decision-making and aggression and minimizes risk—does not develop fully until adulthood.

Half a conversation

Researchers think hearing only half a telephone conversation annoys us because the brain has to work harder to fill in the gaps.

Brain Facts

The brain and the body make an amazing combination, and every day, researchers are learning more and more about how they work together. So many things, such as sneezing, laughing, or getting an irritating song stuck in your head, are just a little bit odd if you stop for a moment and think about them.

Here are some facts for your brain. Exercise your mental processing function and see if you can think of a few more to add to the list.

Laughing

Laughing at a joke uses five areas of the brain as well as mental processing. It starts with an analysis of words and ends with a physical response.

Blinking

You close your eyes to blink, but everything does not go dark. Blinking shuts off part of the brain briefly so you do not notice the bit of darkness.

Sunlight can make you sneeze

Nerve signals triggered by bright light
travel along a crowded nerve path.
If they spill onto other paths, confusing
the signaling, a sneeze may result.

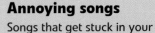

Annoying songs

Songs that get stuck in your
head stay there because the
ability to recall sequences is
a key survival skill. Repetition
cements our memories.

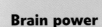

Brain power

A human brain uses about
20 watts of power every day.
That is about half the power
used by a standard
refrigerator lightbulb.

Tickling yourself

You cannot tickle yourself because
your brain distinguishes your touch
from those times when someone
else touches you.

Index

Websites

Due to the changing nature of Internet links, PowerKids Press has developed an online list of websites related to the subject of this book. This site is updated regularly. Please use this link to access the list:

www.powerkidslinks.com/disc/brain/